Voices from the Margins

D1563621

Voices from the Margins

AN ANTHOLOGY OF MEDITATIONS

Jacqui James and Mark Morrison-Reed

EDITORS

Skinner House Books

BOSTON

Copyright © 2012 by the Unitarian Universalist Association. All rights reserved. Published by Skinner House Books, an imprint of the Unitarian Universalist Association, a liberal religious organization with more than 1,000 congregations in the U.S. and Canada, 24 Farnsworth St., Boston, MA 02210–1409.

This project is funded in part by the Fund for Unitarian Universalism.

www.skinnerhouse.org

Printed in the United States

Cover design by Kathryn Sky-Peck
Text design by Jeff Miller

print ISBN: 978-1-55896-671-0
eBook ISBN: 978-1-55896-672-7

6 5
22 21 20

Library of Congress Cataloging-in-Publication Data

Voices from the margins : an anthology of meditations / Jacqui James and Mark Morrison-Reed, editors.
    p. cm.
ISBN 978-1-55896-671-0 (pbk. : alk. paper) — ISBN 978-1-55896-672-7 (ebook)
  1. African American Unitarian Universalists. 2. Meditations.
I. James, Jacqui, 1937– II. Morrison-Reed, Mark D., 1949–
  BX9833.48.A47V65 2012
  242—dc23
                                                2012002522

A vision for Unitarian Universalism in a multicultural world:

With humility and courage born of our history, we are called as Unitarian Universalists to build the Beloved Community, where all souls are welcome as blessings, and the human family lives whole and reconciled.

—UUA Leadership Council, October 1, 2008

Contents

An Invitation

Our Questions

Our Journey

Our Identities

Our Resolve

Our Sources of Strength

Our Seasons

Our Place in the Web of Life

Our Prayers

Foreword

This collection of reflections and aspirations invites us to listen to voices that have been silenced in the past. This kind of listening is vitally important to our religious movement. In order to create a beloved community—one that shares a powerful love and shapes a common purpose—we must know one another. In order to know one another, we must hear each other's stories, see the world through each other's eyes.

I ask us all to listen carefully and attentively to the voices in these pages. I ask that we listen with an open heart for the human experience that lies behind the words. Suspend judgment; just take in the words.

I ask that we also listen deeply. Take time. Reflect. Listen again.

Finally, share these words with others. Use them as readings at gatherings or in worship. Discuss them.

Let every voice be truly and lovingly heard. Let us listen with special attention to those voices that have been on the margins.

—Rev. Peter Morales, President
Unitarian Universalist Association

Introduction

The make-up of the Unitarian Universalist ministry has undergone astounding changes over the past fifty years. For women and LGBTQ ministers, the increase has been nothing less than revolutionary. The change in our ministry's racial and cultural composition has also been significant, but more gradual. In 1962, the year after the American Unitarian Association and the Universalist Church of America consolidated, there were just seven non-Euro-American ministers: John Burciago, whose heritage is Mexican; Andrew Kuroda, who had been born in Japan; and five African Americans, Lewis A. McGee, Ben Richardson, Eugene Sparrow, William R. Jones, and Jeffrey W. Campbell. No one who self-identified as Native American was in ministerial fellowship. Today there are sixteen ministers of Hispanic descent, eight of Native American heritage, thirty-one from the African Diaspora, as well as twenty-four others with South Asian, Japanese, Iranian, Palestinian, Chinese, Korean, and Pacific Islander heritages—plus others who do not fit in any narrow cultural or racial category. Indeed, many of these individuals claim, and try to live in ways that honor, multiple identities. Their reality, as Rev. Leslie Takahashi Morris proclaims, embraces multiple truths, speaks of *both* and of *and*. Living in the borderlands, being neither this nor that, fitting neither here nor there, they speak with unique voices, and offer perspectives that are, at the same time, unusual and universal.

Jeffrey Campbell, the only one of the five African-American ministers at consolidation who had been raised in the faith, characterized his skin tone as "protective coloring." This must sound surprising. While growing up as a mixed-race child in 1920s America, Campbell's color would hardly seem like protection. But he said it rescued him then—and today it still saves those who follow in his steps—from blindly embracing the status quo. Now, as then, skin color does not protect a person from assault and rejection, frustration and pain. Repulsed, Campbell cultivated compassion; treated unfairly, he became attuned to injustice in ways others were not; seeing hypocrisy, he lived up to his ideals rather than settling for what was expedient.

Like Jeffrey Campbell, the contributors in this collection view America from its margins. Therefore, they cannot help but see what many do not. Direct and provocative, but ultimately turning toward hope, the cadence of their voices challenges and then comforts.

As we assembled this collection, we could not help but hear the voices of today's ministers echoing Campbell and their other predecessors. Familiar themes emerged: questioning, being called into community, perseverance, identity, justice, and resolve. They invited us to arrange these writings accordingly.

Over the years, many Unitarian Universalists have told us how useful they have found *Been in the Storm So Long*—the meditation manual which introduced them to the timbre of UU African-American voices. We hope that this collection will be just as useful, perhaps even more so. As you hear these voices, we encourage you to feel the strength of their commitment to transforming our Association into the welcoming, diverse religious home so many of us yearn for it to be. As the number of people of color in our movement has gradually increased, such voices have too often been unheard. Here they speak unwaveringly and powerfully. As Rev. Jonipher Kwong says, "Our voices must be heard. We shall no longer be silent."

This collection speaks—sometimes explicitly and often implicitly—about, from, and to the experiences of people of color in our faith. It reflects our increasingly more diverse ministry and indicates that Unitarian Universalism is striving to address and attract those not presently part of our beloved community. Offering resources that speak to the experiences of those identity groups is key to drawing and retaining a more multicultural membership. If newcomers do not see their life experiences held up and honored by liberal religion, it is unlikely they will find anything compelling about its message. We hope this collection furthers the process of honoring more diverse life experiences in our faith and encourages others to create new, rich, and exciting worship resources that lead us into tomorrow.

—Jacqui James and Mark D. Morrison-Reed

An Invitation

Waiting

Step into the center
    come in from the margins
I will hold you here.

Don't look back
        or around
feel my arms
    the water is rising.
I will hold you
as you tremble.
I will warm you.

Don't look out
        or away
life is in here
    between you and me.

In this tiny space,
where I end and you begin
    hope lives.

In this precious tiny space
no words need be whispered
to tell us we are one.

You and I
          we make the circle
if we choose to.

Come
          step in
I am waiting for you.

—Marta I. Valentín

Come, Come

Come, come, whoever you are
Come with your hurts, your imperfections,
    your places that feel raw and exposed.
Come, come, whoever you are
Come with your strengths that the world shudders to hold
come with your wild imaginings of a better world,
come with your hopes that it seems no one wants to hear.

Wanderer, worshipper, lover of leaving
we will make a place for you,
we will build a home together.
Ours is no caravan of despair.
We walk together;
Come, yet again come.

—adapted from Rumi by Leslie Takahashi

Each Day

Each day provides us with an opportunity to love again,
  To hurt again, to embrace joy,
  To experience unease,
  To discover the tragic.
Each day provides us with the opportunity to live.

This day is no different, this hour no more unique than the last,
Except . . . Maybe today, maybe now,
  Among friends and fellow journeyers,
Maybe for the first time, maybe silently,
We can share ourselves.

—Kristen Harper

River Call

Between rocking the boat
and sitting down;
between stirring things up,
and peaceably going along,

We find ourselves
here,
in community.

Each called
from many different
journeys,
many different
life paths,
onto this river road.

Some are here
because the rocking of
the boat
has been too much:

too much tumult,
too much uncertainty,
too much pain.

Some are here with questions
about where the boat is going;
how best to steer it;
where this journey ends.

Others are here
as lovers of the journey,
lovers of life itself.

Here in front
beside
behind

each a passenger;
each a captain;
doing the best we can.

"Rest here, in your boat,
with me," the river calls;

"Listen to how I flow,
the sound of life coursing all around you."

Let the current
hold you,
let the current
guide you;
the river that gently flows
through your soul,
whispers:
"Come, let us worship."

—Manish K. Mishra-Marzetti

Our Voices Must Be Heard

Spirit of Life,
You speak to us from the East and the West
You speak to us from the North and the South
You call to us from the depths of our being
We respond with enthusiasm and fervor
We cry out from Manila to Maui
We shout from Alaska to Alabama
We proclaim your wondrous love from the highest mountain
    to the deepest ocean
Our voices must be heard. We shall not be silent.
Our voices must be heard.

—Jonipher Kwong

Our Questions

We Are Called

We are all called.
Called by the wind, the rushing water, the fireflies, the
summer sun.

Called by the sidewalk, the playground, the laughing children,
the streetlights.
Called by our appetites and gifts—our needs and challenges.

Called by the bottle, the needle, the powder, the pill, the
game, the bet, the need,
the want, the pain, the cure, the love, the hope, the dream.

Called by the Spirit of Love and Hope, and visions of God's
purpose for our lives.
We are all called.

What do we choose? How do we answer?

—Natalie Fenimore

It Is That Time and That Place

Now is the time to call on the memories of the ancestors who thought they could not walk another step toward freedom—and yet they did.

It is that time and place to call on the memories of the ancestors who, when the darkness of their lives threatened to take away the hope and light, reached a little deeper and prayed yet another prayer.

It is that time and place to remember those who came through the long night to witness another sunrise.

It is that time and place to remember the oceans of tears shed to deliver us to this time, to remember the bent knees and bowed backs, to remember the fervent voices asking, begging and beseeching for loved ones sold off.

Time to remember their laughter and joy, though they had far less, and little reason for optimism, yet they stayed on the path toward a better day.

Time to hold to the steadfast hands and hearts and prayers of the ancestors that have brought us this far.

Time to make them proud and show them, and ourselves, what we are made of.

Time to show them that their prayers and sacrifices and lives were not in vain and did not go unnoticed, nor have they been forgotten.

Did you not know that this day would come?
Did you not know that we would have to change places?
Did you not know that just as our ancestors were delivered that you would also be delivered?

Have you not seen the greatness and power of the Creative Energy in the Universe called God that moves and has its being through human agency?

Have you not seen God in your neighbors' faces? In the homeless? In the battered woman? The trafficked child? The undocumented worker? The dispossessed? It is that time and that place to know that it is our turn, that we must leave a legacy for our children. And all the children.

It is that time and that place.
We are the ones we've been waiting for!
For that, let us be eternally grateful.
Amen and Blessed Be.

—Qiyamah Rahman

Borderlands

I am continually astounded by people who point to the struggle for the rights of African Americans in the 1960s and say that we have done nothing comparable since. They somehow slept through the farm workers' struggles and the gender wars of the seventies, the sanctuary movement of the eighties, and the fight for gay and lesbian rights in the eighties and nineties, all of which still go on today.

They don't make the connection that the bravery Rosa Parks showed when she refused to give up her seat on the bus is the same kind of bravery our gay and lesbian brothers and sisters must call forth just to hold hands with their lovers in public.

It's the same fight! It's the same fight for respect and dignity for every human being. And it's a religious fight, a fight about what's important in the world: to love your brother and sister as yourself; and to love your god, the mystery, the universal, the spirit of life and love, the symbol of all that is good and holy in the world, that which is beyond our knowing, but is the grandest of all—to love that with all your heart and all your soul!

Religions are far from infallible. There are transient elements in the way we worship, and boundaries which we cannot or will not yet see—or confront—as people of faith. These are the borderlands, places where we are challenged by the different and strange. What do we find difficult to see? Who among us has the vision? What revelations hover in our hearts and minds? These are the edges of the future.

—Susan Manker-Seale

Who Is Welcome?

Everybody wants a seat at the table: Blacks, Latinos, Asians, the poor, the disabled, gays and lesbians. Where are all the straight white moderate men supposed to sit? I'm not prejudiced, I am just asking. And what table are they talking about? My table only seats eight comfortably and I have service for ten. That's it. You'll just have to wait your turn. Can you imagine if we just let anyone sit at our table? Why we might have people who can't tell their salad fork from their dinner fork, or people who eat with their hands. I shudder to think.

Anyone is welcome at my table, in my home, as long as you don't have grease stains on your clothes and have washed your hands before you touch my silverware.

Everyone is welcome at my table—as long as you don't try to proselytize me to your religion or your politics. And don't get upset when I question yours. After all, it wasn't my faith that taught me to eat Jesus and drink his blood. Come on in, I say, but don't make fun of my pan-African sculpture and paintings mixed with chintzy curio Precious Moments figurines.

If you don't dress up and don't have every hair in place and you don't smell too fresh, you are welcome, but don't sit on the good leather, or the new futon cover. Here, let me get you a towel. I am told the outside shower works very well.

Everyone is welcome at my table as long as you sit still and don't wiggle or interrupt the grown-up conversations . . . children should be seen and not heard, but they should be dressed up in bows and satin so they can entertain us. Don't worry if they aren't talented, it only reflects on your upbringing, not mine.

Truth is. I don't really have the room for you—maybe next time.

—Kristen Harper

Labyrinth

Walk the maze
within your heart: guide your steps into its questioning curves.
This labyrinth is a puzzle leading you deeper into your own
   truths.
Listen in the twists and turns.
Listen in the openness within all searching.
Listen: a wisdom within you calls to a wisdom beyond you
and in that dialogue lies peace.

—Leslie Takahashi

Our Journey

On the Brink

All that we have ever loved
and all that we have ever been
stands with us on the brink of all that we aspire to create:
a deeper peace,
a larger love,
a more embracing hope,
a greater generosity of spirit,
a deeper joy in this life we share.

—Leslie Takahashi

As We Move

As we move through life
finding ourselves,
always newly wise and newly foolish,
we ask that our mistakes be small
and not hurtful.
We ask that as we gain experience
we do not forget our innocence,
for they are both part of the whole.

—Orlanda Brugnola

Lessons from a Car Radio

Years ago, when my former car (rest its soul) turned ten, it developed an unpredictability and surliness often associated with adolescence. In the beginning it was just little things, like a rash of burned-out headlight bulbs and rogue seat adjustments, but the one quirk that really got on my nerves was the radio. It turned on and off at will, and seemingly at whim. At first it would just take a while until the car warmed up before it started working. Later it would turn on when I started the car, and go off a few minutes later, then back on later still. For a while it worked when it was hot—and then it worked when it was cold. Basically it came on and went off whenever it felt like it.

Over a period of ten years, I learned a lot of things from my car radio—like all the words to "Achy Breaky Heart," and the fact that I still remembered all the words to every song from the sixties, although I could barely remember my own phone number. But during the four years I was in seminary I stuck pretty much to National Public Radio, and since I often drove up to three hours a day I learned a lot from my radio. The greatest lesson though, was this: Never get attached to an NPR story because you never know when the radio is going to turn off.

This lesson—repeated many times in the years since—was a lesson in letting go.

My radio acted as a Buddhist master, teaching me not to become attached to the state of things as they are, or to a particular outcome. I haven't given up hoping for the best. But I've come to realize that while sometimes the outcome I crave is formed from high-minded ideals based on experience, reason and research, other times it's just what I want. And when what I want doesn't happen, it's like Galinda says in the stage show *Wicked*, "Something's terribly wrong. I'm not getting my way."

The challenge for me is to see the longer view beyond my limited perspective. It helps to remember that life is impermanent and imperfect. This, coupled with the faith that everything is innately connected, reminds me that clinging to particulars is both futile and unnecessary.

There's one other thing that I've learned from my car radio. When I graduated from seminary, three churches within commuting distance of my home were looking for ministers. They were all prestigious pulpits, and they were not looking for someone fresh out of school. The night after I received the third rejection letter, I headed out to a meeting at my internship site, feeling dejected and blue. When the car started, the radio was silent. And then, about two minutes into the trip, it turned on, to give me half a line from the Moody Blues' "Nights in White Satin." The words said, "I love you." I know it was only the car radio, but somehow I believed it.

—Jackie Clement

Marginal Wisdom

They teach us to read in black and white.
Truth is this—the rest false.
You are whole—or broken.
Who you love is acceptable—or not.
Life tells its truth in many hues.
We are taught to think in either/or.
To believe the teachings of Jesus—OR Buddha.
To believe in human potential—OR a power beyond a
　　single will.
I am broken OR I am powerful.

Life embraces multiple truths, speaks of *both*, and of *and*.
We are taught to see in absolutes.
Good versus evil.
Male versus female,
Old versus young,
Gay versus straight.

Let us see the fractions, the spectrum, the margins.
Let us open our hearts to the complexity of our worlds.
Let us make our lives sanctuaries, to nurture our many
　　identities.

The day is coming when all will know
That the rainbow world is more gorgeous than monochrome,
That a river of identities can ebb and flow over the static,
    stubborn rocks in its course,
That the margins hold the center.

—Leslie Takahashi

Our Identities

Song of the Universe

For each child that's born,
a morning star rises
and sings to the universe
who we are.

Listen carefully . . .
Can you still hear the song?
The one sung for you
when you were born.
The song sung by a cosmos
in motion
rejoicing at your life.

You, the result.
You, the outcome.
You, the celebration.

Listen carefully . . .
Can you hear it still?
A song of possibility.

A reminder that
we still have time
to be who and what
we need to be.

Listen carefully . . .
The vast expanse
echoes a recognition
that it's not always easy.
Possibilities
can be hard to pursue.

Roads not taken,
wrong turns,
destinations that disappoint.
Through this,
the song persists.
The universe sings no less
because time and space
wear us thin.

The music calls us
to recognize our limitations,
to recognize that

the song is best
sung with others.

Here in community,
bringing alive
that most primordial
and original impulse,
the desire to sing
to the universe who we are,
to celebrate and share
our lives with others.

—Manish K. Mishra-Marzetti

Redskin

Whenever I swim in the ocean
for any bit of time
she emerges with me,
long hair streaming.

Red of the redskin,
brown of the oppressed
flowing down my body
like slow water.

They ask, "Who am I"
to be so dark?

She has always been here
though you couldn't, wouldn't see.

She walks with me for a while
proud and beautiful
"Don't forget me!" she says,
and we promise one more time.

—Susan Manker-Seale

An American Flag Upon My Tasbee

It is a custom, superstition, decoration
to hang prayer beads from the rear-view mirror.
Not broken bodies of long ago prophets,
    not agony in the name of God
    not sculpted, miniaturized terror.

Just beads.

Mine are brown like coffee beans.
Smooth for running through fingers.
Hung for decor they tell
those who would decode
. . . something middle eastern.

Not for faith,
for culture.

So it is no sacrilege
that the smooth brown beads
break their rhythm for a cold metal rectangle of
Red, White, and Blue.

An Announcement!
An American Drives This Car!

When I called I said:
      Don't wear black today—
      it makes you look too ethnic.
      Put away your turtlenecks.
      Choose your pink izod.
He said:
      I told your sister the same,
      and stay away from airports.
      Drive if you have to be somewhere.

      You, he said, are white enough
      you don't have to worry.

Then he said—
      But you do have your American flag
      on your tasbee?

                    —Mitra Jafarzadeh

I Too Am Beautiful

My inner spirit wrote: "I have spent my life watching you, seeing your accomplishments, living the way I think you want me to. I have watched the way you move and the way you talk. I have listened to your story and learned your history. I have sat patiently as you explained your politics, your religion, your philosophy of life. I have walked with you on a journey of faith waiting for my turn to share, to explain, to lead."

Look at me—I am black and you are white, but I too am
    beautiful
Look at my face, my hair, my clothes—they may be different
    but aren't they worthy of your gaze?
Look at my walk, the way my hips sway to the music in my
    soul,
    the way my proud neck tilts to the sun, yes look at me
Look at my darkness, it contains light and love, rebirth and
    growth
Look at my pain, don't turn away
Look at the way you see me, I am human, I have tears and
    fears,

I have laughter and joy
Look at me and walk with me
I too am beautiful.

—Kristen Harper

Exquisite Sight

I watch you
Floating through night,
Knowing your presence
By your flashing eyes,
Your ebony beauty
One with the embracing night.

I see you
Melting in sunlight,
Mingling honeyed tones
With sun's warm glow
On golden sands,
Your maize beauty
One with the enhancing light.

I glimpse you
Drifting at twilight
Across marooned spaces
Where light and dark meet
In somber tapestries,

Your amber beauty
One with the exquisite sight.

You . . . beautiful . . . Black
One with the Universe.

—Yvonne Seon

Thali

I have stuck it out in this faith, even through doubt and deep ambivalence, because this is the way I want to live my life. My Unitarian Universalism lets me live out my Hindu faith; it helps me be a better Hindu, and a better human being.

I stay because Unitarian Universalism has a healing message for a broken world yearning for reconciliation and wholeness.

I stay because Unitarian Universalism is committed to working through race and class, homophobia and ableism, though we have much to learn and far to go.

I stay to celebrate my multi-hyphenated identity, not so much as an American melting pot but rather a South Indian thali—a selection of tasty dishes in different bowls presented on a single plate. Each dish tastes different, and does not necessarily mix with the next. They belong together because they complement each other in making the meal a satisfying repast.*

---

*Adapted from a reference by Sashi Thardoor in his essay, "The Idea of India."

I stay to find the strength to live honestly among the various interstices of my life; to take responsibility for the ambiguities of my pluralistic identity while seeking common ground with others.

—Abhi Janamanchi

One Love

We are one,
A diverse group
Of proudly kindred spirits
Here, not by coincidence—
But because we choose to journey—together.

We are active and proactive
We care, deeply
We live our love, as best we can.

We ARE one
Working, Eating, Laughing,
Playing, Singing, Storytelling, Sharing and Rejoicing.
Getting to know each other.
Taking risks
Opening up.
Questioning, Seeking, Searching . . .
Trying to understand . . .
Struggling . . .
        Making Mistakes

Paying Attention . . .
       Asking Questions
Listening . . .
       Living our Answers
Learning to love our neighbors
Learning to love ourselves.

Apologizing and forgiving with humility
Being forgiven, through Grace.

Creating the Beloved Community—Together
We are ONE.

—Hope Johnson

Our Resolve

Having Been the Other

May what we know of suffering, redemption and salvation
    bring us to Love.
Having been the *other*, may our hearts exclude no one.
Having been the slave, may we long to be no one's master.

                    —Natalie Fenimore

Social Justice

Many people use the term *social justice* in self-serving ways; what they mean by social justice is "just us."

But social justice can only begin with the interaction between fortunate people and those who are disadvantaged. It is incumbent upon those who, by virtue of the accident of birth or other circumstances, have good jobs, good educational background, and good lives, to come to the assistance of those who face formidable obstacles to getting an education and leading fulfilling lives.

Social justice insists that people are not their circumstances; they are their possibilities. Social justice demands that all people, regardless of their birth circumstances, are entitled to a fair chance at life, that every person has the right to life, liberty, and the pursuit of happiness.

—Donald E. Robinson

Prayer for Living in Tension

If we have any hope of transforming the world and changing
  ourselves,
we must be
bold enough to step into our discomfort,
brave enough to be clumsy there,
loving enough to forgive ourselves and others.

May we, as a people of faith, be granted the strength to be
so bold,
so brave,
and so loving.

—Joseph M Cherry

Are We Living in a Post-Racial World Yet?

We get good at what we practice. Research now tells us very clearly what distinguishes amateurs from experts—it's the amount of time they spend practicing their craft.

To become exceptional, you must do two things. First, you must practice with intention—you have to aim to become very good. If you set out just to know how to do something or do it "good enough" then that is how good you will become. To become expert, you have to envision yourself as a master of your craft.

Second, you must practice a lot and consistently. Studies show that amateurs practice about three times a week for about an hour per sitting. Those who develop into experts put in three hours a day almost seven days a week. They become consumed with their craft.

In addition, there is a magic number. Becoming an expert demands about ten thousand hours of practice! That's twenty hours a week every week for about ten years.

The notion of intentional practice also applies to how we become the beloved community. It's not enough to just say that we are post-racial, we have to practice being post-racial.

It is said that if you're not on the court, you're not in the game. We have to put in the time on and off the court.

—Xolani Kacela

Saving Unitarian Universalism

The thing that will save our faith, and that will allow us to become better lovers, fathers, mothers, daughters, sons, and friends, is building relationships—learning more about each other—seeing God in all people, places, and things. It's rooted in experience. The more we learn and grow with liberal minds and hearts, the more we see the Spirit emanating. The more we learn about our common destiny, the more we see that we all come from the same source; that we are all capable of good; that "God don't make no junk"; that the world we have is the world we've collectively created through our thoughts, words, and deeds. And when we see things differently, we start doing things differently.

—John T. Crestwell Jr.

Nada te Turbe (Don't Despair)

Faith doesn't mean believing in god. Faith is having trust in your sense of the rightness of the universe. Hope is clinging to that trust in the direst circumstances. Love is deciding to care for this world no matter what horrors come our way. Thus we keep despair at bay. And when we add a daily dose of laughter, we are on the road to healing.

—Susan Manker-Seale

Bless a Stranger with a Smile

Take time each day to remember you are a part of the interconnected web of life. Bless a stranger with a smile. Tell the people in your life how much they mean to you. And take a moment every day, beginning today, to give thanks for all that you have.

May you have the strength, courage, and commitment to begin or continue the rewarding journey of self-understanding. May you have the wisdom to forgive yourselves, the grace to ask for forgiveness, and the compassion to forgive others.

You are the co-creator of your life. It's up to you. Forgive your trespasses as you forgive those who trespass against you. May you live your beliefs and feel at one with everyone and everything.

Blessings upon you,
Blessings upon me,
Blessings upon every living thing,
Blessed Be.

—Monica Cummings

Our Sources of Strength

The Three Jewels

We take refuge in all that is holy.

We take refuge in sacred teachings throughout the ages.

We take refuge in our community of faith and in the
interdependent web of life.

—Jonipher Kwong

Love Abundant

I lift my eyes up to the hills
from where will my help come?
My help comes from Love abundant.
my help comes from the hills
my help—my help, it comes from
ancient Mothers whose hearts beat in mine.
It comes from the trees that sway and the breeze that sways
them . . .
my help comes from all that was and is and will ever be . . .
I lift my eyes . . . hushed by the soothing touch of waves
caressing wounded shores
wounded souls
I lift my eyes . . . to the horizon bathed by
the hum of mothers and mothers' mothers
cradling—gently rocking
I lift my voice—call of the sea trees sister moon mother
earth
my soul weeping—a symphony of life overflowing
I give myself
I too hum through every pore

with every breath
I give myself—
an extension
of all that is, was, and ever will be.

—Alicia R. Forde

God's Tears

I sometimes think the stars are God's tears. Even God's sorrow creates sources of great illumination, joy and beauty through these celestial bodies. At our very best, we human beings are microcosms, containing within us sparks of divinity. Sometimes I think my own heart, shattered by sorrows, is like a cascade of diamonds. Each piece is valuable and radiant, a source of joy and illumination to beings known and unknown to me, as the stars are a source of strength and radiance to me, although I am unknown to them.

—Shuma Chakravarty

History's Road

Source of Life,

The road of history is long, full of both hope and disappointment. In times past, there have been wars and rumors of wars, violence and exploitation, hunger and homelessness, and destruction of this earth, your creation.

We have become a global village, with a growing realization of how fragile this earth is, and how interconnected we are to each other and to all creation.

We cannot continue to live in the old way. We must make a change, seek a new way. A way toward peace with justice and a healthy planet.

O Great Creative Spirit: You have given a vision of the good, and we yearn for a new way. But where are we to find the courage to begin this work? We know that a different tomorrow is possible, but how can we build it?

We think of the prophets, women and men, who voiced unpopular opinions, who made personal sacrifices, and sometimes lost their lives, for the sake of justice.

We think of Isaiah, who called out to let those who are held in captivity go free, to give solace to the poor and homeless. Let us be inspired by all who work to overcome misery, poverty, and exploitation.

We think of Harriet Tubman, who called out to people of good will to join her on an underground railroad, to lift a dehumanized people from the bondage of slavery to the promise of freedom, even when it meant challenging unjust laws. Let us be inspired by those who are outlaws for freedom.

We think of Gandhi, whose belief in "Soul Force"—the witness to Love's Truth—helped to overthrow the oppression of an empire and gave witness to the way of nonviolent action. Let us be inspired to become witnesses for peace.

We think of Chief Seattle, who reminded us that we belong to the earth, not the earth to us. Let us be inspired by all those who work for the healing of creation, of Mother Earth and all her creatures.

Who are the prophets who inspire you? They may be well known, or known only to you, offering personal inspiration, courage, and hope.

May they join a great cloud of witnesses to a new way of life—the way of peace and justice, the way of justice lived according to the way of peace, the beloved community.
So may it be. Amen.

—Clyde Grubbs and Marjorie Bowens-Wheatley

Faith and Belief

Last summer my husband, John, and I were canoeing in New Hampshire. At the end of a trip around the lake I climbed out of the canoe first, had one foot in the lake and one foot in the canoe. That's when things went wrong. While taking my foot out of the canoe, I caught my heel on the edge. Losing my balance, I instinctively reached for the most solid thing within my grasp—the canoe. There are times when grabbing on to what appears most solid and stable is exactly the wrong thing to do. When I resurfaced, I saw my husband sitting in a foot and a half of water fishing for his glasses on the lake bottom. In my attempt to save myself, I took an innocent bystander down as well.

I tell this story not to demonstrate my lack of boating expertise, but to say that I understand the emotional impetus to grab onto what seems most stable and solid when the world is tipping us off our feet. In religious terms, we might say we are driven to hold ever more tightly to our beliefs when we are under stress.

Like grabbing a canoe for stability, depending on belief to keep us from going under is to grasp at the wrong thing. It is not our belief that we need to hold onto, but our faith. Though the two are often taken to mean the same thing, there is a subtle and critical difference. *Faith* is a deeply seated confidence, vital to our very existence; *belief* is only what we think is true, though we wouldn't stake our lives on it. Faith leaves room for mystery, belief does not. As Albert Einstein wrote in his personal credo, "The most beautiful emotion we can experience is the mysterious."

Sometimes what seems most solid and stable is only an illusion of stability. Things that appear more ethereal, that may seem to be the toughest to grasp, are in fact the most stable and secure. Love, faith, and community may seem to be intangible ideals, but if nurtured they can serve as the very bedrock of our lives.

Beliefs can fall away. But the things that seem most insubstantial—perhaps because they can be the hardest to come by—have the greatest worth, and provide the steadiest base.

—Jackie Clement

Our Seasons

Ground of Being

Knowing ourselves radiant,
May we know God radiant
Beautiful as a clear-eyed child
Blinding us in glory.

Knowing ourselves dark,
May we know God dark
Beautiful as sun-kissed skin
Fertile as the deep rich earth.

God of the Earth,
Spirit of Life,
You are for us as the ground is for seed.
Warm and nurturing,
You are our sacred birthplace.
In you we sprout, take root, and grow;
Like growing seeds, may we live into our radiance,
Our possibilities, our imaginings, and our love.

—Natalie Fenimore

Suddenly One Summer

Suddenly one summer
I stepped off the shores of America
The home of the brave and the land of the free
And found my way back
To where my spirit used to be

Suddenly one summer
My memory returned
I heard the call of the sea
Mother waited on the Gold Coast
I came face to face with me

Suddenly one summer
I relived four hundred years
The deafening screams dying on air
With pain and suffering
And no one to care

Suddenly one summer
My eyesight returned
I cried for lost sisters and brothers

I cried for myself
And I cried for the others

Suddenly one summer
I let go and reclaimed
I found myself
My home, my name
Suddenly one summer

—Addae A. Kraba

Harvest Time

Let us ground ourselves
in this season,
ground ourselves
in this time and space.

Winter is near upon us;
our last task before it
is the harvest.

Seeds have yielded all manner of fruit,
all manner of consequences.
We enter this sacred space
bringing our whole selves,
the parts we like
and the parts we do not.

We come together,
each with our own harvest,
seeking here a word
of comfort,

an experience of beauty,
inspiration to guide us.

Let us ground ourselves
in that purpose,
ground ourselves
in body and soul.

Winter is near upon us;
sunlight gives way to night,
the coldness grows closer.
Gathering together, we
seek warmth
in one another's company,
seek the eternal light
that permeates all.

Whatever your harvest,
whatever your pain or joy,
here you are welcome
and will be held.
Let the warmth flow to you
and through you;

feel the healing strength
of this community.
Know that here you are not alone,
that here you have found
companions for the journey.
Grounded in that spirit,
grounded in the spirit of thanksgiving.
Come, let us worship.

—Manish K. Mishra-Marzetti

In Gatherings

In gatherings we are stirred
like the leaves of the fall season
rustling around sacred trees,
tossed hither and yon
until we come to rest together,
quietly, softly . . .
We come to gather strength from each other.
We come to give strength to each other.
We come to ask for strength from the Spirit of All That Is
    and Is Not.

When our hearts sing or when they frown
it is the way of compassion telling us to give.
It is the way of peace telling us
to share our gifts,
for we are happiest
and most powerful
when Love is made apparent
in and through us.

Spirit of the circle that is Love,
as we twirl in this dance that is life
we give thanks for reminding us each day
of our task of ministering to each "other"
with a searching glance,
a safe touch,
a generous smile,
a thoughtful word . . .

Thank you for reminding us
that we are always building our beloved *comunidád*.

Thank you for reminding us
that through our covenant with you
we covenant with each "other"
and are made whole.

In gratitude, we celebrate
with open hearts and minds.
We discover who we are,
separate from each other
and within one another.

In this circle that holds all life
may we ever work toward
widening its boundaries
until there are none.

Amen. Paz. Blessed Be.

—Marta I. Valentín

This Holiday Season

Let this holiday season be a time for engaging heart to heart.

For those who, like the innkeeper, turned us away;
For holidays that didn't live up to our expectations.

For ghosts of Christmas past that haunt us;
For those who gave us gifts, but never their presence.

For gifts we yearned for, but did not receive;
For things we received, but never wanted.

For those who offered us cheer when we needed comfort;
For those who offered us love that we could not accept.

For those we rejected, offering no room in our homes or
    hearts;
For ourselves, who could not give through fear.

For the times we saw a star in the East, but failed to follow it;
For times we followed the star, but it did not lead where we
    hoped.

For miracles gone unnoticed;
For wise men and women, whose gifts we rejected.

All these we remember, we forgive, we love.

In doing so, may we be granted an abiding peace.

—Addae A. Kraba

When Snow Falls Gently
Reminding Me of You

In the late hours
when snow falls
gently
covering the broken ground,
and boards,
and twisted roots,
and cans,
and bottles,
the world is smooth
when snow falls gently.
I see your face chasing away the bitter cold.
Hold me close,
rock me in your loving arms,
sing lullabies that help me remember.
Teach me to turn back to my snow-driven self,
dancing in the rapture of my first breath,
singing to the sound of music and arts,
moving to the poetry of rhythm in motion
that fills my heart every time I think of you,
my Beloved One.

Then I remember:
I don't need to return,
I never left.
You and I are one,
dancing in silky smoothness,
beating back the cold with the rhythm of our dance steps,
filling the world with laughter
as the cold winds blow and our hearts,
like burning embers,
become the warmth of the sun carried on the winds.

—Om Prakash

Our Place in the Web of Life

Reformation: The Spirit of the Wind

Some say the spirit of the wind is in the trees.
     You can see it, they say,
If you close your eyes and stand real still.

Some say that the same spirit lives in the hills
     Forging mountains and plains.

I smelled it the other night.
Lying in my bed, my window cracked
     It crept through the moonlight
     Up under my blanket
And wrapped its arms around me.

Entering my blood through my skin
I felt alive with an age I had not yet reached.
     Made new again in a form I'd never known.

I cried out in pain and joy mingled,
Fear and expectation.
     Ecstasy it has been called,
     I call it reformation.

There was forgiveness in that spirit
Compassion for my wounds,
Strength for my weaknesses.

It was no miracle, nor nirvana.
    I just closed my eyes and saw the spirit.

The spirit in the wind.
The spirit in the trees.
The spirit that lives in me.

—Kristen Harper

Mālama 'Āina

In Hawaiian, *mālama* means "to care for" and *'āina* means
"the land." We are admonished to care for the Earth because
the Earth has shown great care for us by providing us with food,
shelter, and healing energy. Each year, millions come to Hawaii
to find rest, comfort, and nurture for their overworked bodies
and tired spirits. They come to be connected to the *'āina* and
the transformative power it offers. But to simply receive these
gifts without offering something in return robs us of a recip-
rocal relationship with the Earth. *Mālama 'āina* means par-
ticipating in beach clean-ups, recycling, installing solar panels,
and being mindful of our carbon footprints. *Mālama 'āina* is a
way of being that ensures the web of life remains vibrant and
healthy. If we *mālama* the *'āina*, the *'āina* will *mālama* us.

—Jonipher Kwong

A Riff

I came as rain
a droplet from the sky
splashing
returning
to sisters and brothers.
A trickle
then a rivulet.
A cascading stream
following
the course of least resistance.

Pond
    Rapids
Lake
    River
Growing deep
and powerful
placid and powerful.
Flowing
into the ocean

and
a silence
that is not an end.

I came as a cloud shading those I loved,
dew that glistened and evaporated,
tears coursing down,
waters of joy and gratitude.
Life's precipitation
can't be captured
or contained,
only kissed.

—Mark D. Morrison-Reed

The Stars Are Dancing

The stars are dancing tonight,
while the moon sits in her golden hammock,
swaying back and forth
to the rhythm of celestial voices.

The Beloved is full of rapture,
dancing worlds and stars into being,
drunk with the wine of passion
and filling the heavens with song.

Do not sit alone in the dark
while creation sings three-part harmony.
Dance, my friends.
Dance wildly,
sing joyfully,
fill your heart with the beauty of the Beloved
as the Beloved turns your soul to light.

—Om Prakash

A Beautiful Assortment

Our galaxy is one little speck among trillions of specks in the universe. Like the lines on a zebra or the human fingerprint, no two galaxies appear to be exactly alike. There are varying solar systems and planets, and many suns, in these galaxies, each with different dimensions.

We live in an expansive and diverse universe. But you don't have to go to outer space to learn that lesson. Right here on earth there are millions of species of all types—animals, insects, trees, plants, and sea creatures. There's fresh water and salt water, blue water, green water; tropic and arctic climates. And then there are the people—all types, with varying languages and customs. Life is a beautiful assortment! We have much to celebrate.

—John T. Crestwell Jr.

All We Are One

Each of us comes from a different place, yet all we are one.
We carve for ourselves our own unique space, yet all we
    are one.
We learn how to speak, eat, dress, cook, and play in
    different ways.
Of common homeland, we have not a trace, yet all we
    are one.
We kill, maim, and harm one another with no thought
    for God's will.
We forget the One God and one grace, yet all we are one.
On a mountain in East Africa near Olduvai Gorge, our
    common mother, "Eve,"
Says that we come from one human race, and all we
    are one.

—Yvonne Seon

Our Prayers

What Is Prayer?

What is prayer?

Perhaps it is easier to define what prayer is *not*.

Prayer is not a recitation of fantasies, cravings, and demands. Prayer is not a monologue in an echo chamber. Prayer is not ventriloquism nor self-hypnosis. Prayer is not dreamy wishing or wishful thinking.

What, then, is prayer? It is God's continuing gift to Creation. Prayer is our grace-given ability to contact the Creator immediately, without intermediary or interruption. Our soul is the divine spark within our flawed and fractured beings, a spark that remains radiant, unpolluted by our errors, for the soul is of God. Through genuine prayer, we commune with our Creator and find what we really need, not necessarily what we erroneously desire, for our sojourn on this narrow bridge of life between eternity and infinity—the unknowns that precede birth and succeed death.

In our mortal life, prayer is the most powerful gift God has given us to contact our Source—to aid and empower us on this mysterious voyage.

—Shuma Chakravarty

For Those Who Pray
and Those Who Don't

For those who pray and those who don't,

For those who believe there is some ultimate power that listens and can affect the world,
And, for those who believe that it is only through the power and love of our own hearts that we make a difference,

We pray to ourselves, to each other, to God, Goddess, Spirit, the Great Mystery of the Universe that is beyond our understanding as well as our naming,

Within each of our hearts is a yearning, a yearning for something better for ourselves, for each other, for the world.

That is our prayer.

Beyond the personal prayers of our hearts, we share the collective prayers of humanity, prayers for love and justice, mercy and solace, respect, compassion and peace. Universal prayers manifest in the values we cherish.

Prayer is the seed, the guide, the vision, the direction. But our hands must work to build a better world and our feet must walk the paths that lead to a universal, loving, respectful human community.

Let us pray, and then, let us begin the work, once again.

—Susan Manker-Seale

Let It Be Done

Dear Unknown, Unknowable, Yet Known by Many Names

Keep us mindful that we are all related. That when one of us
　　is ignored and treated with dis-ease, we all suffer.
Today let each of us commit to welcome the stranger.
Let us move beyond our comfort zones and connect with people
　　labeled *different* and pushed to the edges of society.
We can make a difference.
We can transform lives.
We can bring harmony and healing to the places and spaces
　　where we live, work and play.
Let us keep our hearts and minds open and receptive to the
　　still, small voice that calls us to stand witness for those
　　who cannot stand,
to speak the truth for justice for those without a voice
and to lead the way on the journey toward wholeness for
　　those without sight.
In the spirit of love, compassion and community, let it be done.
Blessed Be.

—Monica Cummings

We Dream of Peace

Loving Spirit
of this and every sacred moment,
be with us in times of self-doubt
when we forget that dreams are not born in an instant
but must be nurtured,
must be chosen over and over.
When the world is telling us that we are dreaming too large,
too wild, too unrealistic, or even
too small . . .
remind us, gentle, patient Spirit,
that any dream worth waiting for
is worth working toward.

Precious and Loving God,
today more than ever
we dream of peace—
peace in our hearts, which have been
clouded over with promises
of a free world
that will never come to pass
if bought with the blood of war.

Dear God, today we dream of peace . . .
today we dream of peace.
Amen.

—Marta I. Valentín

Traditional Hindu Prayer

May good befall all.

May there be peace for all.

May all be fit for excellence.

May all experience the holy.

May all be happy.

May all be healthy.

May all experience what is good.

May no one suffer.

—translated and adapted by Abhi Janamanchi

Only Begun

Spirit of Life and Love, dear God of all nations:
There is so much work to do.
We have only begun to imagine justice and mercy.

Help us hold fast to our vision of what can be.
May we see the hope in our history,
and find the courage and the voice
to work for that constant rebirth
of freedom and justice.
That is our dream.
Amen.

—William Sinkford

Our Work Is Not Yet Done

O, Spirit of Life and Love that lives within us and among us, be with us now. Help us take our history into our hearts as well as our minds. Open us, so that we can feel our past live in us— the joy, the disappointment, the passion, the pain, the hope. Let the past, all of it, live in the core of our being.

Let us be humble. Let us be honest. Help us to take instruction from our past. And let us also be inspired. But more than anything, let us feel your spirit, the spirit of deep compassion, here among us this very moment.

O, Spirit of Love and Life, help us to know, truly know, that we are your people, bound together by our collective memory and, more importantly, by our shared aspirations. We are not perfect. We mess up. Sometimes we talk too much. Yet we are drawn together by what we love, by what we hold sacred and by a vision of what we may yet create together.

Finally, tender and gentle Spirit, guide us. Inspire us. Embolden us. For our work, your work, O Spirit, is not yet done.

—Peter Morales

About the Contributors and Editors

MARJORIE BOWENS-WHEATLEY (1949–2006) served as minister to Unitarian Universalist congregations in New York City and Tampa, Florida. She also served as the adult programs director for the Unitarian Universalist Association and as an anti-racism consultant and trainer for the UUA and for the Metro New York district of the UUA. She was a contributing author of three books: *Essex Conversations: Visions for Lifespan Religious Education*; *Interdependence: Renewing Congregational Polity* (the 1997 report of the Unitarian Universalist Association Commission on Appraisal); and *Weaving the Fabric of Diversity*. She also co-edited *Soul Work: Antiracist Theologies in Dialogue*. Marjorie earned degrees from American University and Wesley Theological Seminary. She served as a member and chair of the UUA Commission on Appraisal, as a board member of the Unitarian Universalist Women's Federation, and was a founding member of the African American Unitarian Universalist Ministry (AAUUM). Prior to working in ministry, Marjorie had an accomplished career in public broadcasting and media.

ORLANDA BRUGNOLA is proud to be a multi-racial person of Chinese descent. Her father, born in Italy, with a Chinese grandmother, emphasized the gift of being "Eurasian." He knew about China's history, culture, medicine, literature, and values. Orlanda studied Mandarin and calligraphy in her childhood and retained strong Confucian values. Though her father knew little about his great-grandfather's African culture, he taught her deep respect for it. She wishes that more of her mother's German and Irish heritage had been conveyed to her. Her Confucian upbringing asserts itself more strongly as she gets older and she is resuming her study of Mandarin. She is bilingual in French and English.

SHUMA CHAKRAVARTY is a Unitarian Universalist minister who has served both Unitarian Universalist and United Church of Christ churches. She is currently the director and minister of the Resource Center of Ecology, Compassion and Culture based in Cohasset, Massachusetts. She was born and raised in Kolkata, India. Her maternal and paternal ancestors were among the founders and leaders of the Brahmo Samaj. She has lived in the US since 1971 but has travelled globally. She has graduate degrees from Simmons College in

English literature and from Boston University and Harvard University in theology. She has published poetry and prose in several anthologies. Shuma regards herself as an international, multicultural, interfaith pilgrim journeying to the One. Some of her heroes are her mother, Uma Devi, Mother Teresa, Coretta Scott King, Yvonne Egdahl, Tagore, Gandhi, and the Dalai Lama. The Unitarian Universalist ministers who have inspired her most are the late Rhys Williams, Michelle Bentley, and Mark Morrison-Reed.

 JOSEPH M CHERRY grew up as a multi-racial kid of Mexican and Polish descent in Metro Detroit. He earned an undergraduate degree in American history from the University of Illinois in Chicago, focusing on Protestant religious movements and gender and women's studies. He received a graduate degree from Meadville Lombard Theological School and was ordained by his home congregation, First Unitarian Society of Chicago. He has served congregations in Chicago, Vancouver, and Dukinfield in England. When not working in his current position as interim minister at the Unitarian Universalist Fellowship of Stanislaus County in Modesto, California, Joe enjoys square dancing, quilting, photography, and life with his beloved, Rev. Denis Paul.

JACKIE CLEMENT serves as senior minister of the Unitarian Universalist Church of Bloomington-Normal, Illinois. She earned an MDiv from Andover Newton Theological School and served congregations in Maine and Massachusetts before moving to Illinois. Prior to entering the ministry, Jackie worked in the high-tech industry as an engineer and marketing manager for computer graphics systems. She is co-author, with Alison Cornish, of *Faith Like a River: Themes from Unitarian Universalist History*, a curriculum from the Unitarian Universalist Association's *Tapestry of Faith* program. She is also the author of "Time/Money Balance" in the UUA's *Taking It Home* series, a resource for families. Her passions include history, cooking and reading, but the visual arts continue to be her primary spiritual practice. She celebrates her Latina heritage through food, language, and the arts. She lives in Normal with her husband, John Ford.

JOHN T. CRESTWELL JR. is the associate minister of the Unitarian Universalist Church of Annapolis, Maryland. He formerly served as minister of Davies Memorial Unitarian Universalist Church in Camp Springs, Maryland, which he helped expand into a multiracial congregation. He currently serves on the Unitarian Universalist Association President's Council and as the director of outreach of the Unitarian Universalist Legislative Ministry of Maryland. He was formerly a board member of the Unitarian Universalist Legislative Ministry of Maryland, of UMR Communications in Dallas, Texas, and of the Unitarian Universalist Church of the Larger Fellowship. He has also been an adjunct professor at Potomac College in Washington DC, teaching comparative religion, ethics, African-American history and public speaking. John is the author of *Conversations: The Hidden Truth that Keeps the World from Being at Peace* and *The Charge of the Chalice*. He received a BA in Mass Media Arts from Hampton University and an MA in Theology from Wesley Theological Seminary in Washington DC. He is committed to working for the marginalized and oppressed and is a self-proclaimed Unitarian Universalist evangelist.

 MONICA L. CUMMINGS began working at the Unitarian Universalist Association in October 2008, after serving for more than six years as a parish minister. She received her DMin in pastoral care and counseling at the Claremont School of Theology and is a member of the American Association of Pastoral Counselors. Monica is a proud African

American, and is grateful to have spent twenty-six months working in education and community development as a Peace Corps volunteer in South Africa. She continues her community involvement as the lead facilitator for the Making It Better Now support group for LGBTQ youth and young adults at the LGBT Center of South East Wisconsin. She works with association, district, and regional staff of the UUA; congregational leaders; Diverse Revolutionary Unitarian Universalist Multicultural Ministries (DRUUMM); Allies for Racial Equity (ARE); and multiracial and multiethnic families on programming to support the ministry needs of youth and young adults of color and their allies.

 NATALIE FENIMORE is an African-American Unitarian Universalist minister, currently serving as minister for religious exploration at the Unitarian Universalist Congregation of Fairfax, in Oakton, Virginia. She is president of the Liberal Religious Educators Association (LREDA). Natalie and her family have been members of the Unitarian Universalist Church of Rockville, Maryland, for thirty years.

ALICIA R. FORDE serves as the multicultural congregations program coordinator at the Unitarian Universalist Association. She is a graduate of the Iliff School of Theology and currently lives in Longmont, Colorado. Alicia was born and spent her formative years in Trinidad and Tobago. She identifies as an African-descent, queer, cisgender female, with deep roots in Tobago and will readily admit that there is much about her current identity that reflects her nineteen years of living in the United States. When she's not hiking, you can find her volunteering with Bent Lens Cinema, running, or soaking up the sun.

CLYDE GRUBBS is a Unitarian Universalist minister who has served congregations in Indiana, Quebec, Massachusetts, Texas, Florida, and California. Since August 2010, he has been the minister-at-large of the Tuckerman Creative Ministries for Justice and Healing. Clyde has been a member of the Diverse Revolutionary Unitarian Universalist Multicultural Ministries (DRUUMM) for eleven years and presently serves as one of its co-presidents. He has served on the Unitarian Universalist Ministers Association Executive Committee as its portfolio holder for anti-racism, anti-oppression and multiculturalism. He was recently elected as an at-large member of the Unitarian Universalist Association Board of Trustees. Before entering the ministry, Clyde worked as a community and labor organizer. He has worked for peace, justice and equality ever since he was in the Unitarian Universalist youth movement, Liberal Religious Youth. He honors his Native American heritage, Texas Cherokee, which informs his spiritual understanding and practice as well as his anti-racist and anti-oppressive commitment.

KRISTEN L. HARPER has been serving the Unitarian Church of Barnstable, Massachusetts, as senior minister since 1992. Of West Indian and Russian Lithuanian descent, Kristen was the second woman of African descent to be called to a Unitarian Universalist church through the UUA settlement process. Kristen served congregations in Lansing, Michigan, and Ormond Beach, Florida. She and her husband Jay live in Marstons Mills, Massachusetts, with their four cats. She was educated at Boston University and Meadville Lombard Theological School, where she graduated in 1999 with a DMin.

MITRA JAFARZADEH was born in Lexington, Kentucky, but spent her early years in Tehran, Iran, before moving permanently to the US on the eve of the Islamic Revolution in 1979. Mitra has bounced between Kentucky, Oklahoma, North Carolina, and the Washington suburbs before taking up residence in Farragut, Tennessee, as the called minister of the Unitarian Universalist congregation there. Born to an Iranian father and an Appalachian mother, Mitra was destined for an eclectic existence and unique view on life. She sees herself as either an Iranian-American, or as a Persia-lachian/Appa-persian. She studied sociology and anthropology at the University of North Carolina at Greensboro and attended seminary in Lexington, Kentucky, among the Disciples of Christ. She lives in Tennessee with her two kids, two dogs, and her partially domesticated husband.

JACQUI JAMES is an African-American religious educator who worked for the Unitarian Universalist Association for seventeen years in several capacities, including serving as the staff liaison to the Hymnbook Commission that produced the UUA hymnbook, *Singing the Living Tradition.* She co-authored with Judith Frediani the *Weaving the Fabric of Diversity* curriculum and was deeply involved in the anti-oppression work that transformed the UUA during the 1980s and 1990s. She was active in the formation of both the African American Unitarian Universalist Ministries and the Diverse Revolutionary Unitarian Universalist Multicultural Ministries. She coordinated the Beyond Categorical Thinking program and also served as the UUA's affirmative action officer. Now retired, she is active in her congregation in Newton, Massachusetts, enjoys quilting and spending time with her three grandchildren.

ABHI JANAMANCHI is a native of India. While his father was Muslim and his mother Hindu, he was reared in the Brahmo Samaj, a liberal Hindu tradition similar to Unitarian Universalism. Abhi has served as senior minister at the Unitarian Universalists of Clearwater congregation in Florida since 1999. He and his wife, Lalitha, have two teenage sons, Abhimanyu and Yashasvi. Abhi identifies as a South Asian Indian Hindu Unitarian Universalist.

HOPE JOHNSON is a long-term, active Unitarian Universalist who hails from Jamaica, by way of the world. The expression "there's always hope" conveys much of her optimistic, vision-filled spirit. She is a dreamer who gives life to her dreams by taking action. Her commitment to Unitarian

Universalism is enhanced by her strong cross-cultural and multi-faith life experience. Hope currently serves as minister of the Unitarian Universalist Congregation of Central Nassau in Garden City, New York. She previously served as director of religious education and minister of spiritual growth at First Unitarian Congregational Society in Brooklyn. She is the continental Good Offices person, or "minister to ministers," of the Unitarian Universalist Ministers Association. She also serves the Unitarian Universalist Association as a consultant and trainer in leadership development and anti-racism, anti-oppression, and multiculturalism.

XOLANI KACELA has been a fellowshipped minister in the Unitarian Universalist Association since 2008. He teaches classes for the online doctoral program in Pastoral Community Counseling at Argosy University. He also serves as a chaplain for the Texas Air National Guard and has been deployed several times, including to Iraq. Prior to this, he served as the minister of pastoral care at First Unitarian Church of Dallas, Texas. He has written numerous articles for books, journals, and magazines. He resides in Cedar Hill, Texas. His hobbies include running, indoor cycling, music, and traveling. He identifies as African American.

ADDAE A. KRABA lives in Philadelphia, Pennsylvania, where she serves as consulting minister to the Dorothea Dix Unitarian Universalist Community in Bordentown, New Jersey, and as affiliate community minister to the First Unitarian Universalist Church of Philadelphia. Addae also teaches on an adjunct basis at her alma mater, Starr King School for the Ministry in Berkeley, California. She cites growing up an only child in a multigenerational household of spiritual, creative, African-American women as the foundation for her early interest in the goddess as divine and the formation of her Womanist theology. Addae is herself a mother and grandmother.

JONIPHER KWONG is an ordained minister with the Unitarian Universalist Association and the Metropolitan Community Churches. He currently serves the First Unitarian Church of Honolulu. He is also a member of the Unitarian Universalist Association's Journey Toward Wholeness Transformation Committee. He graduated with an MDiv and a DMin from Claremont School of Theology in California. In addition to his ministerial experience, he has worked in the film industry; at the business consulting firm McKinsey & Company;

and as the executive director of several nonprofits. Though born and raised in the Philippines, Jonipher is ethnically Chinese. In addition to English, he speaks Fookienese and is conversant in Tagalog, Cebuano, Mandarin, and French. He currently resides in Honolulu, Hawaii, and has been with his partner for thirteen years. He enjoys watching cheesy movies, snorkeling in Hanauma Bay and composting as a spiritual practice.

 SUSAN MANKER-SEALE has been a Unitarian Universalist minister for twenty-five years, serving congregations in Phoenix and Tucson. Her father and grandfather were both Unitarian Universalist ministers, and her mother's ancestors make her a fifth-generation Unitarian. Living in the Southwest near Mexico (and in the former Mexican territories) for generations has shaped her cultural leanings and she identifies as Latina. She is bilingual in Spanish and English. Her ancestry is German, Hungarian, and Delaware Native American. She has been married to Curtiss for thirty-two years and they have raised two children, Ben and Katie, to adulthood. Now they have grandchildren. She loves nature and calls herself a mystical naturalist. Lately she has been doing a lot of writing, including fantasy, nature theology, and the occasional poem.

MANISH K. MISHRA-MARZETTI serves as minister of the Unitarian Universalist Church in Cherry Hill, New Jersey. He previously worked as a director of religious education, a high school teacher in religious studies, and a diplomat for the US government under the Clinton administration—working, in part, on human-rights issues. As a Unitarian Universalist of Hindu and Indian-American heritage, he brings an Eastern perspective to his ministry as well as the experience of growing up in an immigrant household. Manish has served the denomination by working on the Unitarian Universalist Association Commission on Appraisal, as a founding member of the Unitarian Universalist Association Council for Cross-Cultural Engagement, and as a former president of the Diverse Revolutionary Unitarian Universalist Multicultural Ministries.

PETER MORALES has served as president of the Unitarian Universalist Association since June 2009. The first Latino president of the UUA, he was elected on a platform of growth and multiculturalism. Public witness is central to his presidency; he is especially passionate about immigration reform and environmental justice. As president, he is responsible to the UUA Board of Trustees for administering staff and programs that serve more than a thousand member congregations. He also acts as principal spokesperson and minister-at-large for the UUA. Prior to his election, Peter served as the senior minister at Jefferson Unitarian Church in Golden, Colorado. From 2002 to 2004, he was the UUA Director for District Services. He also served on the UUA Board of Trustees as trustee from the Mountain Desert District, and on the Unitarian Universalist Ministers Association Executive Committee, as the first person to carry its anti-racism, anti-oppression, and multiculturalism portfolio.

 MARK D. MORRISON-REED was raised in the First Unitarian Society of Chicago, where he was ordained in 1979. He has spent half his life outside the US. Since 1988 he has resided in Toronto and holds dual citizenship in the US and Canada. For twenty-six years he served as a parish minister. He has also served as vice-chair of both the Unitarian Universalist Association Commission on Appraisal and the Ministerial Fellowship Committee, and is a former president of the Canadian Unitarian Council. Currently he is an affiliated faculty member at Meadville Lombard Theological School in Chicago. Mark has written extensively about the African-American experience in Unitarian Universalism.

OM PRAKASH (John Gilmore) is a Life Coach and Wellness Consultant. He was ordained as a Unitarian Universalist minister in 1995 and received his final fellowship in 1998. During his ministry at the Unitarian Universalist Church of Manchester in New Hampshire, he entered a doctoral program at University of Creation Spirituality, writing a dissertation on how to remove the lasting effects of linked-oppression through traditional healing methods such as tai-chi, yoga, massage, Reiki, and spiritual direction. In 2001 he received his DMin in Reinventing Work and Spirituality. He comes from a multicultural family: one grandmother was a Cree, another was a Cherokee; one grandfather was African American and the other was half Cherokee and half African American. As a life coach and wellness consultant, Om Prakash works to facilitate a multicultural understanding of the world and multicultural methods for self-healing and spiritual growth.

QIYAMAH A. RAHMAN has been a Unitarian Universalist since 1992, when she was introduced to Frances Ellen Watkins Harper. Her research has focused on black women in Unitarian Universalism, among other subjects. From 1999 to 2005 she served as district executive of the Thomas

Jefferson district. She was the first African-American woman to hold the position of district executive in the denomination. Currently, she is the director of contextual ministry and senior minister at Meadville Lombard Theological School. A native of Detroit, Qiyamah obtained a BA in Education and an MSW from the University of Michigan; an MDiv from Meadville Lombard Theological School; and a doctorate from Clark Atlanta University in Africana women's studies, with a major in gender and development and a minor in feminist/womanist theory.

DONALD E. ROBINSON is the president and founder of Beacon House, a nonprofit, community-based organization that provides social work services to at-risk children and youth in Washington DC. He was introduced to Unitarian Universalism at All Souls Church, Unitarian, in Washington, where he was a religious education teacher. When he entered the ministry, his goal was to create a program to minister to at-risk youth. In 1991, after graduating from Howard Divinity School and serving an internship with the Unitarian Universalist Church of Rockville, Maryland, he founded Beacon House. The program started with his offering homework help and snacks to a small group of children in one small room.

Twenty years later, Beacon House serves hundreds of children with homework help, meals, sports, mentoring, and cultural activities. Though Donald is the president and founder, today much of the work is done by a cadre of capable staff and volunteers. He is proud of what has been accomplished, but dreams that Beacon House might accomplish even more.

 YVONNE SEON became the Unitarian Universalist Association's first female African-American minister in 1981 when she was ordained at All Souls Church, Unitarian, in Washington DC. From 1989 to 1991, she led an "intentionally diverse religious community" of Unitarian Universalists. She is the author of "Transcending Boundaries," a meditation on diversity first published in the Skinner House meditation manual *Been in the Storm So Long*, and of several articles about her religious journey from Christianity to Islam by way of Unitarian Universalism. An educator and public servant before entering the ministry, Yvonne later returned to university life to work on the development of the black studies curricula. Now retired, she lives in Yellow Springs, Ohio.

WILLIAM SINKFORD is the senior minister of the First Unitarian Church of Portland, Oregon. He served as the seventh president of the Unitarian Universalist Association from 2001 until 2009, the first African American to lead a traditionally white denomination. Previously, he had served as the UUA director of congregational, district, and extension services. Born in San Francisco in 1946, Sinkford was an active member of the First Unitarian Church of Cincinnati, Ohio, during his teenage years, serving as the president of Liberal Religious Youth, the continental UU youth organization. He graduated cum laude from Harvard in 1968. After college, Sinkford worked in the field of marketing, and later housing development, before entering Starr King School for the Ministry, where he earned his MDiv in 1995.

LESLIE TAKAHASHI has been writing since she was five years old and her mother made her start a journal as part of a student teaching experience. She is the co-author, with Chip Roush and Leon Spencer, of *The Arc of the Universe Is Long: Unitarian Universalists, Anti-Racism and the Journey from Calgary* (Skinner House). She has also written for a number of professional publications, and authored unpublished novels and poems. She has also penned an extensive collection of short dramatic works, including a chancel drama about Hosea Ballou, and composed simple meditative songs. Recently she has begun writing more about her experience as a multiracial person with Japanese-American roots. Leslie found Unitarian Universalism in her twenties and has served as minister to congregations in Charlottesville, Virginia, and Walnut Creek, California. Her children, Garner and Liam, offer ongoing inspiration.

MARTA I. VALENTÍN serves First Church Unitarian in Littleton, Massachusetts. Previously, she served in New Orleans during Hurricane Katrina and in Arlington, Virginia. Her poems and prayers have been published in various venues, including most recently in the Skinner House books *Encounters: Poems about Race, Ethnicity and Identity*, edited by Paula Cole Jones, and *The Arc of the Universe Is Long: Unitarian Universalists, Anti-Racism and the Journey from Calgary*, edited by Leslie Takahashi Morris, Chip Roush and Leon Spencer. She identifies as a Latina lesbian and lives in Littleton with her wife Alison, daughter Jaiya, and elderly but young-of-spirit cat Boo. A percussionist, she is working on combining her poetry with her drumming to create "percussive poetry."